F
D
RECIPES

Cold & hot sweets,
desserts and puddings

with illustrations by
Helen Allingham RWS

SALMON

Index

Cover pictures *front: 'A heavy load'   back: 'Mind where you go'*
title page: 'The stile'

Printed and Published by J. Salmon Ltd., Sevenoaks, England © Copyright

Coffee Ice Cream Charlotte

A delicious party sweet consisting of a sponge finger mould filled with rum flavoured coffee ice cream.

**1 tablespoon apricot jam, sieved   20 boudoir biscuits
4 tablespoons bottled coffee essence   4 eggs, separated
3 tablespoons rum   4 oz icing sugar, sifted   10 fl.oz whipped cream
Double cream and toasted almonds to decorate**

Brush the sides of a loose bottom 6 inch round cake tin with the jam. Trim the biscuits to the depth of the tin and stick them to the jam around the sides. Whisk the coffee essence, egg yolks and rum together in a bowl. Beat the egg whites until stiff, fold in the icing sugar, add to the yolk mixture and fold in the whipped cream. Pour into the tin, cover with kitchen foil and freeze until firm. To serve, carefully push up and remove from the tin, transfer to a flat serving dish and decorate the top with whorls of double cream and toasted almonds. Serves 8.

Pear and Orange Caramel

The pears for this dish are poached in a light syrup and combined with orange segments;
they can be given extra flavour by the addition of a little Cointreau to the liquid.

2 lb cooking pears, peeled, quartered and cored
10 fl.oz water   5 oz sugar   4 large oranges

Poach the pears in a syrup consisting of the water and 3 oz of the sugar until tender, but not broken, then transfer to a serving dish. Thinly peel the rind from 2 oranges, cut into thin strips, boil in a little water until tender then drain and set aside. Meanwhile, remove the peel and pith from all the oranges, divide the flesh into segments and mix with the pears in the dish. Chill in the refrigerator until required. Boil the remaining 2 oz sugar with 1 tablespoon water to make a rich brown caramel, then pour on to an oiled plate to set. When set, crush with a rolling pin into small pieces, sprinkle over the fruit and garnish with the softened strips of orange peel. Serve with cream. Serves 6.

Upsidedown Apple Tart

Made with Cox's or similar dessert apples topped with golden caramel,
this tart is derived from the French classic Tarte Tatin.

5 oz sugar   4 tablespoons water   2 oz butter
2 lb Cox's Orange Pippins, peeled, cored and sliced into thickish segments
1 oz caster sugar   1-2 teaspoons brandy   6 oz sweet shortcrust pastry

Melt the 5 oz sugar in a heavy pan with 4 tablespoons water over a low heat until it caramelises to a golden brown. Pour the caramel over the base of a warmed and lightly buttered 8 inch sandwich tin and tilt to spread evenly. Leave to harden. Set oven to 425°F or Mark 7. Melt 1 oz of the butter in a pan and gently cook the apple slices for 2 to 3 minutes until just soft but retaining their shape. Arrange the apples in overlapping rings over the base of the tin. Melt the remaining butter in the pan, add the brandy then pour over the apples. Roll out the pastry on a floured surface, cut to a circle the size of the tin, lay over the apples and press down lightly. Bake for 25 to 35 minutes, checking, and if browning too quickly cover with a piece of baking paper. When cooked, allow to cool for 5 minutes then invert and turn out on to a warmed serving plate. Serve warm with cream. Serves 4.

Savarin Mould

A rum soaked sponge ring, filled with fresh soft fruit and decorated with whipped cream.

4 oz butter, softened   2 large eggs, beaten
4 oz caster sugar   4 oz self-raising flour
SYRUP
3 oz sugar   10 fl.oz water   2 tablespoons rum
FILLING
1 lb fresh fruit (strawberries, raspberries, etc)   5 fl. oz whipped cream

Set oven to 350°F or Mark 4. Well butter a 2½ pint ring mould. In a bowl, cream together the butter and sugar and then add the beaten eggs and flour. Beat well and spoon into the mould. Bake for 20 to 30 minutes then leave to cool in the mould for 5 minutes before turning out on to a wire rack. Allow to become completely cold. SYRUP: Dissolve the sugar in the water in a pan over a low heat and then boil for 3 minutes. Add the rum and set aside to cool. When the syrup mixture is only just warm, pour over the savarin. Place the savarin on a serving dish, fill the centre with the soft fruit as desired and pile on the whipped cream. Serves 6.

Mocha Chiffon Cake

A light textured chocolate and coffee gateau covered with cherry jam and whipped cream.

2 oz cocoa powder	3 large eggs, separated
4 tablespoons hot strong black coffee	1½ oz melted butter
3 oz self-raising flour	10 fl.oz whipped cream
Pinch of salt	2 oz plain chocolate, grated
6 oz caster sugar	Black cherry jam

Set oven to 350° F or Mark 4. Grease the base of a spring-formed 8 inch round cake tin and line with non-stick paper. Blend together the cocoa powder and coffee and leave to cool. Sift the flour and salt into a bowl. In another bowl, combine the sugar and egg yolks and beat until pale, then stir in the melted butter and the cocoa/coffee mixture. Gradually fold the mixture into the flour, using a metal spoon. Beat the egg whites until stiff and fold in to the mixture until evenly blended. Pour into the tin and place the tin on a baking sheet. Bake for 45 to 60 minutes or until a skewer inserted comes out clean. As soon as the cake is out of the oven, turn the tin upside down on a wire rack and leave until quite cold. Then, carefully remove the tin from the cake, spread a good layer of cherry jam on top, completely cover with whipped cream and sprinkle with grated chocolate. Eat the same day as made. Serves 10 to 12.

Rum and Chocolate Flan

An uncooked biscuit based flan filled with a rum flavoured custard.
This recipe contains an uncooked egg white.

BISCUIT BASE
3 oz butter   3 level dessertspoons golden syrup   6 oz crushed digestive biscuits
FILLING
1 egg yolk   2 oz caster sugar   5 fl.oz milk
1 tablespoon rum   1 egg white, stiffly beaten
¼ oz gelatine sprinkled over 1 tablespoon hot water
DECORATION
5 fl. oz whipped cream   4 glacé cherries, halved   Grated chocolate

Butter a 7 inch flan dish. Melt the butter and syrup together gently in a pan, add the biscuit crumbs and mix well. Allow to cool slightly before pressing firmly on to the base and sides of the flan dish. Chill while making the filling. Whisk together the egg yolk, sugar and milk in a bowl over a pan of boiling water (but not touching) until it thickens. Allow to cool. Fold in the rum, the egg white and the dissolved gelatine. Mix until quite cold and then pour into the flan case and chill. When set, decorate with a ring of cream topped with cherries and scatter grated chocolate over the centre. Serves 6.

Amaretto Delights

A very quick and easy cold sweet made with Italian almond flavoured liqueur.

1 oz blanched almonds　　**1 oz caster sugar**
10 fl.oz double cream　　**4 tablespoons Amaretto liqueur**
Amaretti macaroons or small ratafia biscuits

First, toast the almonds under a medium grill until golden brown and then chop finely. In a bowl, whip together the cream and sugar and then blend in well the Amaretto liqueur. Divide the cream into 4 individual sundae glasses, sprinkle with the toasted chopped almonds and refrigerate until required. Serve with Amaretti macaroons or small ratafia biscuits. Serves 4.

Apple and Orange Tart

A tangy fruit tart glazed with orange marmalade.

8 oz sweet shortcrust pastry
1½ lb cooking apples, peeled, cored and sliced   4 oranges
2 oz sugar   ½ teaspoon ground cinnamon   ¾ oz flour
4 oz orange marmalade, melted

Set oven to 375°F or Mark 5. Grease an 8 inch flan tin. Roll out the pastry on a floured surface and line the flan tin. Poach the apple slices in a very little water until just soft but retaining their shape. Peel the oranges, remove the pith and cut the flesh into slices. Mix together the sugar, cinnamon and flour. Arrange the apple and orange slices in layers in the tin, dusting each layer with the sugar mixture. Finish with a layer of orange slices. Brush the melted marmalade over the top and bake for 30 to 40 minutes until firm and golden. Serves 4 to 6.

New College Pudding

Not really a pudding but a type of fritter; these small suet puddings, fried in butter, have been traditional at New College, Oxford since the early 19th century.

4 oz shredded suet	**4 oz currants**
4 oz white breadcrumbs	**1 oz chopped candied peel**
2 oz sugar	**3 eggs, beaten**
½ oz baking powder	**1 tablespoon brandy**
Pinch of salt	**Butter for frying**
Caster sugar for sprinkling	

In a bowl, mix together the suet, breadcrumbs, sugar, baking powder and salt with the currants and peel. Next, stir in the beaten eggs and brandy. The mixture should have a soft, dropping consistency. Heat sufficient butter in a pan and fry spoonsful of the mixture for about 6 minutes until brown, turning once. Serve hot, sprinkled with caster sugar. Serves 6 to 8.

Fruit Crumble

An easy to make, every day sweet for which any type of soft
or hard fruit can be used according to season.

1 lb prepared fruit   **4 oz butter**
7 oz caster sugar   **½ lb flour**

Set oven to 375°F or Mark 5. Prepare the uncooked fruit according to the type used and arrange in a greased ovenproof dish, layering the fruit with 4 oz of the sugar. In a bowl, rub the butter into the flour until the mixture resembles breadcrumbs and then stir in the remaining 3 oz sugar. Sprinkle the mixture over the fruit and press down well. Bake for 35 to 40 minutes until the topping is lightly browned, reducing the oven temperature slightly after 15 minutes. Serve with custard or cream and extra sugar if necessary. Serves 4 to 6.

Strawberry Cream

A light summer dessert made from strawberries and cream.

1 lb ripe strawberries   6 oz sugar
1 pint double cream, lightly whipped
1½ oz gelatine   5 fl.oz hot water

First beat the strawberries to a pulp, then stir in the sugar. Pass the mixture through a sieve and then fold in the lightly whipped cream. Dissolve the gelatine in the hot water, allow to cool and blend into the fruit/cream mixture, stirring until it begins to set. Pour into a wetted mould and leave to set completely. When required, stand the mould in warm water for a minute and turn out. Alternatively, serve in individual sundae glasses. Serves 6.

North Country Tart

*An open tart layered with raspberry jam topped with
an egg, coconut and golden syrup mixture.*

8 oz shortcrust pastry	**1 oz caster sugar**
2 tablespoons raspberry jam	**1 oz golden syrup**
2 oz butter	**4 oz desiccated coconut**

1 small egg, beaten

Set oven to 375°F or Mark 5. Grease an 8 inch pie plate. Roll out the pastry on a lightly floured surface and use to line the pie plate, trimming the edge. Spread the raspberry jam over the base. Gently melt the butter, sugar and golden syrup together in a pan over a low heat. Remove from the heat and stir in the coconut and beaten egg. Combine well together and spread out over the jam. Bake for 25 to 30 minutes or until the filling is set and the pastry golden. Serve hot or cold with double cream. Serves 4 to 6.

Orange Pudding

A light, orange flavoured steamed pudding.

4 oz butter, softened	2 tablespoons milk
4 oz caster sugar	1 oz white breadcrumbs
2 eggs, beaten	$\frac{1}{2}$ teaspoon baking powder
4 oz self-raising flour	Grated rind and juice 1$\frac{1}{2}$ oranges

Butter a 2 pint pudding basin. Cream together the butter and sugar in a bowl until light and fluffy. Beat in the eggs and fold in the flour. Add the milk, breadcrumbs, baking powder and orange rind and juice and beat thoroughly. Put the mixture into the basin and cover and seal with greaseproof paper and kitchen foil. Steam for 1$\frac{1}{2}$ to 2 hours topping up the water as necessary. Turn out and serve with custard or warmed light jelly marmalade. Serves 4 to 6.

Butterscotch Meringue Pie

A pastry case filled with butterscotch mixture topped with baked meringue.

8 oz shortcrust pastry
FILLING
3 oz butter   4 oz light soft brown sugar   1 tablespoon water
2 oz flour   15 fl. oz milk   2 egg yolks   3-4 drops vanilla essence
TOPPING
2 egg whites   3 oz caster sugar   1 tablespoon granulated sugar for sprinkling

Set oven to 350°F or Mark 4. Grease an 8 inch flan dish. Roll out the pastry on a floured surface and use to line the flan dish. Prick the bottom and bake blind for about 20 minutes. FILLING: Put 1 oz of the butter into a pan, add the sugar and water and heat gently until the sugar dissolves; do not boil. Set aside. In a second pan melt the remaining 2 oz butter, add the flour and stir. Add the milk and bring to the boil, stirring continually, boil for about 5 minutes then stir in the caramelised sugar from the first saucepan. Allow the mixture to cool before adding the egg yolks and vanilla essence, then beat well and pour into the pastry case. Reduce oven to 325°F or Mark 3. TOPPING: Put the egg whites into a clean bowl and beat until they form soft peaks. Fold in the caster sugar with a metal spoon. Pile the meringue on top of the pie mixture, sprinkle with granulated sugar and bake for 20 to 30 minutes until pale gold. Serve hot or cold. Serves 6.

Plum Mousse

A light, frothy cold dessert made with plum purée flavoured with port wine.

1 lb plums   Finely grated rind 1 lemon   2 teaspoons lemon juice
2 tablespoons sugar (or more to taste)   3 level teaspoons gelatine   5 fl.oz hot water
1 tablespoon port wine   10 fl.oz double cream   2 egg whites
Whipped cream and flaked almonds to decorate

Wash the plums, put into a pan with the lemon rind and juice and the sugar with just a very little water and cook until soft. Remove the stones and put through a sieve to purée the flesh. Dissolve the gelatine in the hot water then stir into the warm plum purée and set aside to cool but not set. Then stir in the port wine. Whip the cream until it just holds its shape and fold in to the purée. Whisk the egg whites until they stand in soft peaks and fold in. Put the mixture into a 2 to 2½ pint fancy mould or into a glass serving bowl and refrigerate until set. When required, stand the mould in warm water for a minute and turn out. Decorate either the mould or in the bowl with rosettes of whipped cream 'spiked' with almonds. Serve with boudoir or cat's tongue biscuits. Serves 4 to 6.

Spiced Peach Pudding

A spicy sponge filled with halved peaches and with a crunchy sugar topping.

3 oz butter, softened   3 oz caster sugar   2 small eggs
2 oz self-raising flour   1 oz ground almonds   1 teaspoon ground cinnamon
3 fresh peaches, peeled, stoned and halved (if using tinned peaches, drain well)
1 tablespoon Demerara sugar with ½ teaspoon ground cinnamon for sprinkling

Set oven to 375° F or Mark 5. Lightly butter a 9 inch flan dish. Cream together the butter and sugar in a bowl until light and fluffy. Then beat in the eggs and fold in the flour, ground almonds and 1 teaspoon of cinnamon. Spoon the mixture into the dish and spread out. Arrange the 6 peach halves, cut side down, over the sponge mixture and press down. Mix ½ teaspoon cinnamon with the Demerara sugar and sprinkle evenly over the pudding. Bake for about 30 minutes until golden. Serve warm with whipped cream. Serves 4 to 6.

English Trifle

Unlike many of the trifles made today, this is a truly traditional trifle made with a creamy egg custard and flavoured with brandy and sherry.

8 trifle sponges	**15 fl.oz milk**
½ lb raspberry or apricot jam	**5 fl.oz double cream**
Ratafia or macaroon biscuits	**8 egg yolks**
2 fl.oz brandy	**3 oz sugar**
6 fl.oz sherry (as available)	**10 fl.oz whipped cream**

Ratafia biscuits, split blanched almonds, glacé cherries and angelica to decorate

Slice the sponge cakes, spread them with jam and arrange over the base of a glass serving dish. Lay a few ratafia biscuits or macaroons over the sponge, pour over the brandy and sherry and leave to soak for at least 30 minutes. Beat the egg yolks with the sugar in a bowl. Heat the milk and cream to blood heat in a pan and pour over the egg mixture and blend together. Strain into a bowl and place over a pan of boiling water (but not touching) and stir until thickened. Allow to cool slightly then pour over the sponge cakes. Leave the trifle to set and, when cold, pipe with the whipped cream and decorate with the ratafia biscuits, almonds, cherries and angelica. Serves 8.

Bread and Butter Pudding

This recipe gives an extra dimension to an old favourite.

1½ pints milk	**4 large slices white bread**
Grated rind of 1 lemon	**2 oz butter**
4 eggs	**½ oz currants**
2 oz sugar	**½ oz sultanas**
2 tablespoons brandy	**½ oz chopped mixed peel**
1 teaspoon vanilla essence	**Grated nutmeg for sprinkling**

Set oven to 350°F or Mark 4. Heat the milk with the lemon rind in a pan and leave to steep for 10 minutes. In a bowl, beat the eggs with the sugar, brandy and vanilla essence, strain the milk into the eggs and mix well. Butter the bread slices, remove the crusts and cut into triangles. Butter a pie dish and arrange half of the currants, sultanas and peel over the bottom. Arrange half of the bread pieces over the fruit then cover with the remaining fruit. Pour half the custard over the bread and leave to soak for 5 minutes. Arrange the remaining bread slices on top, pour over the remaining custard and dust with grated nutmeg. Bake in a *bain-marie* for 45 minutes until set and browned. Serve hot with cream. Serves 6.

Orange Liqueur Sorbet

*A soft, water ice which makes a refreshing party dessert
either served on its own or with fruit salad.*

**8 oz caster sugar   1 pint water
Grated rind and juice 1 large orange
2 tins mandarin orange segments, drained
2 tablespoons lemon juice   6 tablespoons apricot brandy
2 egg whites, stiffly beaten**

In a pan, dissolve the sugar in the water over a gentle heat, add the orange rind, bring to the boil and boil for 10 minutes. Set aside until quite cold. Liquidise the orange segments in a food processor, add the orange juice, lemon juice and brandy and stir into the cold sugar syrup. Pour into a shallow, rigid container and freeze until half frozen. Turn out into a bowl and beat until mushy. Fold in the beaten egg whites, return to the freezer container and freeze until solid. Serves 6 to 8.

Almond Pudding

A delicately flavoured rich custard pudding.

15 fl.oz milk	**6 oz ground almonds**
5 fl.oz double cream	**1 teaspoon rose or orange flower water**
2 oz white breadcrumbs	**3 eggs, beaten**
3 oz sugar	**1 oz butter for dotting**

Set oven to 350º F or Mark 4. Butter a 2 pint pie dish. Warm together the milk and cream over a gentle heat and pour over the breadcrumbs in a bowl. Stir in the sugar, ground almonds and flower water and leave to soak for about 15 minutes. Beat the eggs in a bowl, add the milk/breadcrumb mixture and blend together thoroughly. Pour into the pie dish and dot with butter. Bake in a *bain-marie* for about 30 minutes until set. Serves 4 to 6.

Apple Fritters

Fruit fritters can be made with very many varieties of fruit. Apples are the most usual, but bananas, pineapple rings and orange slices, etc. are alternatives.

Dessert apples, peeled, cored and cut into ½ inch thick rings
BATTER

4 oz flour	**1 dessertspoon olive oil**
Pinch of salt	**4 fl.oz tepid water**
2 egg whites	

Sieve the flour and salt into a bowl, make a well and add the oil. Pour in most of the water and gradually beat in the flour. Add the remaining water if necessary, but keep the batter stiff as the egg whites will thin it down. Cover and leave in a cool place for about 1 hour. When the batter is required for use, whisk the egg whites until stiff and fold in. Coat each ring (or piece of prepared fruit) with batter, using a spoon and fry in deep hot fat. Keep warm on a dish until all the fritters are made then sprinkle with caster sugar and serve.

Pumpkin and Apple Pie

*Pumpkins are available from October to December, so this is a
useful autumn dessert; especially at Hallowe'en.*

¹/₂ lb prepared pumpkin (peeled and de-seeded)
¹/₂ lb prepared cooking apples (peeled, cored and diced)
4 oz currants   1 teaspoon mixed spice   1 oz chopped mixed peel
1 lb puff or ¹/₂ lb sweet shortcrust pastry
Caster sugar for sprinkling

Set oven to 425°F or Mark 7. Butter a large pie dish. Cut the pumpkin flesh into ¹/₂ inch cubes and mix with the apple dice, currants, mixed peel and spice. Arrange the mixture in the pie dish. Roll out the pastry on a floured surface and cover the dish, trimming and decorating with surplus pastry. Moisten the pastry with water and sprinkle thickly with caster sugar, pressing it down lightly. Bake for 10 to 15 minutes then lower oven to 350°F or Mark 4 and bake for about 30 minutes more until golden brown. Serve with double cream or custard. Serves 6.

Eve's Pudding

This baked apple pudding is so called for obvious reasons. It can be made with other fruits but it is then not a true Eve's Pudding, which must be made with apples.

4 oz butter, softened 4 oz caster sugar
2 eggs, beaten 4 oz flour Pinch of salt
1½-2 lb apples, peeled, cored and thinly sliced
4 oz sugar 2 cloves

Set oven to 375° F or Mark 5. Butter a 2 pint ovenproof dish. Cream together the butter and sugar in a bowl until light and fluffy. Then beat in the eggs and fold in the flour and salt. Arrange half the apple slices over the base of the dish, cover with the 4 oz sugar, add the cloves and finish with the remaining apple slices. Spoon over the creamed mixture and spread out evenly. Bake in the oven until the mixture is set and lightly golden. Serves 6 to 8.

Peach Delight

A simple trifle dessert using tinned peaches and a jam swiss roll.

1 pint sweetened custard	**4 gingernut biscuits, crushed**
1 plain jam Swiss roll	**5 fl.oz whipped cream**
1 large tin peach halves	**6 glacé cherries**

First make 1 pint of sweetened custard. Cut the swiss roll into 6 slices and arrange over the base of a shallow, rectangular dish. Spoon 6 tablespoons of the liquid from the peaches over the cake slices and then pour over the warm custard. Set aside until completely cold. Arrange the peach halves, cut side up, on the custard in two rows. Sprinkle the biscuit crumbs around the peaches. Pipe a whorl of cream in the centre of each peach and top with a cherry. Keep chilled until required to serve. May be made in 6 individual glass dishes, if preferred. Serves 6.

Everlasting Syllabub

This delicate dessert will, unlike most syllabubs, hold its shape for about twelve hours.

10 fl.oz white wine	**1 lemon**
1 tablespoon medium sherry	**2 oz caster sugar**
2 tablespoons brandy	**10 fl.oz double cream**

Pour the wine, sherry and brandy into a bowl. Peel the lemon very thinly and squeeze out the juice. Add the peel and juice to the wine mixture, cover and leave to stand in a cool place overnight. Next day, remove the peel and discard. Add the sugar to the wine mixture and stir until dissolved. Pour in the cream and whip until the mixture stands in soft peaks. Spoon into 4 tall glasses or sundae dishes and serve with boudoir or cat's tongue biscuits. Serves 4.

Ginger Pudding

A steamed sponge pudding topped with golden syrup
and incorporating chopped stem ginger.

4 oz butter, softened	**4 oz self-raising flour**
4 oz caster sugar	**2 oz stem ginger, chopped**
2 eggs, beaten	**3 tablespoons golden syrup**

Butter a 2 pint pudding basin. Cream together the butter and sugar in a bowl until light and fluffy. Beat in the eggs and fold in the flour and chopped ginger. Put 3 tablespoons syrup in the bottom of the basin and spoon in the sponge mixture. Cover and seal with greaseproof paper and kitchen foil and steam for 1½ to 2 hours, topping up the water as necessary. Turn out and serve with custard. Serves 4 to 6.

Sherry Cream

A rich, creamy lemon and sherry flavoured custard. An individual party dessert.

15 fl.oz milk	**8 egg yolks**
5 fl.oz double cream	**3 oz caster sugar**
Grated peel of 1 lemon	**2 fl.oz sherry**
Whipped cream to decorate	

Gently heat the milk and cream together in a pan over a low heat, add the grated lemon peel and set aside, covered, to infuse for about 15 to 20 minutes. Beat the egg yolks and sugar together in a bowl, pour in the infused milk, blend thoroughly and strain. Stir in the sherry and cook in a double saucepan, or in a bowl over a pan of boiling water (but not touching) until it thickens. Spoon into individual custard cups or ramekin dishes and chill. Before serving, decorate each custard with a swirl of whipped cream. Serve with sponge fingers. Serves 8.

Mincemeat Layer Pudding

This unusual steamed pudding is made up of layers of suet crust pastry and mincemeat.
Jam or chopped fruit with sugar can be substituted for the mincemeat if preferred.

8 oz flour	**4 oz shredded suet**
½ teaspoon salt	**Cold water to mix**
½ teaspoon baking powder	**Mincemeat**

Sift together into a bowl the flour, salt and baking powder and mix in the suet. Mix to an elastic dough with just enough water to leave the sides of the bowl cleanly. Roll out the pastry on a floured surface to about ¼ inch thickness and cut out rounds to fit the basin. Put a layer of mincemeat in the bottom of the basin, cover with a circle of pastry and continue layering, finishing with a pastry layer on top. Cover and seal with greaseproof paper and kitchen foil and steam for 2 to 2½ hours, topping up the water as necessary. Turn out and serve with custard. Serves 4 to 6.

Orange Fool

A simple but luxurious cold dessert for a summer party.

Sponge cakes, as required
Grated rind and juice 4 oranges
Grated rind and juice 2 lemons
3 oz caster sugar   1 pint double cream
Crystallised orange and lemon slices to decorate

Cut sponge cakes into ½ inch strips, sufficient to line the base and sides of an approx. 2½ pint decorative serving dish. In a bowl, mix the rind and juice of the oranges and lemons with the sugar, until the sugar is dissolved. Next, whip half of the cream until thick but not stiff and slowly beat into it the mixed fruit juices. Spoon the cream mixture over the sponge cakes, put into the refrigerator to chill and leave until the sponge cakes have absorbed the cream and it has set. Whip the remaining cream to stiff peaks and pipe decoratively on top of the fool. Decorate with crystallised orange and lemon slices. Serves 6 to 8.

Rice Pudding

Rice pudding is one of the oldest "nursery" type puddings and the inclusion of suet in this recipe gives it an especially creamy texture.

2 oz short grain pudding rice
Pinch of salt
1 oz caster sugar

½ oz shredded suet
1 pint milk
1 oz butter for dotting

Grated nutmeg for sprinkling

Set oven to 300°F or Mark 2. Butter a 1½ to 2 pint pie dish. Wash and drain the rice and put it into the dish with a small pinch of salt, the sugar and the suet. Stir in the milk and dot with butter. Bake towards the bottom of the oven for about 1 hour, then stir in the skin, grate a sprinkling of nutmeg over the top of the pudding and continue baking for about another hour until set and the skin is lightly browned. Serve on its own or with jam or cream, as preferred. Serves 4.

Lemon Meringue Pie

A flan with a tangy lemon filling topped with meringue. It can be served hot or cold.

6 oz shortcrust pastry
FILLING
2 level tablespoons cornflour   4 oz caster sugar
Grated rind and juice 2 large lemons   Pinch of ground nutmeg
5 fl.oz water   2 egg yolks   ½ oz butter
MERINGUE
2 egg whites   4 oz caster sugar

Set oven to 375°F or Mark 5. Grease an 8 inch flan tin. Roll out the pastry on a floured surface and use to line the tin. Prick the base and bake blind for 20 to 25 minutes until cooked through. In a bowl, blend the cornflour, sugar, lemon rind and nutmeg with a small amount of the water until smooth. Heat the remaining water in a pan, pour over the blended mixture, return to the pan and cook for one minute, stirring constantly. Allow to cool then mix in the egg yolks, butter and lemon juice and pour into the baked pastry case. MERINGUE: Whip the egg whites until stiff, add half the sugar and beat again. Fold in the remaining sugar and spread over the top of the lemon mixture. Bake for 15 to 20 minutes and serve at once. If the pie is to be eaten cold, bake at 325°F or Mark 3 for about 50 to 60 minutes to allow the meringue to harden. Serves 6.

Coffee Cream Cake

A sponge mixture cake, heavily soaked in a coffee and brandy syrup and covered with double cream. A luxurious party dessert.

6 oz butter, softened   6 oz caster sugar
3 large eggs, beaten   6 oz self-raising flour   Pinch of salt
SYRUP
8 oz granulated sugar   15 fl.oz water   2 tablespoons rum or brandy
3 tablespoons bottled coffee essence
TOPPING
10 fl.oz double cream, whipped   Glacé cherries, hazelnuts and grated chocolate

Set oven to 350ºF or Mark 4. Grease and line the base and sides of a deep 8 inch round cake tin. In a bowl, cream together the butter and sugar, add the beaten eggs, flour and salt and mix well. Put into the tin, level the top and bake for about 40 to 50 minutes until firm and a skewer inserted comes out clean. Leave in the tin for 15 minutes then turn out on to a large dish. SYRUP: Gently heat the sugar and water together in a pan until dissolved. Remove from the heat and stir in the rum or brandy and the coffee essence. Prick the top of the cake all over with a skewer and pour over the hot syrup mixture; the cake must be warm. Leave the cake for at least 12 hours to absorb the surplus liquid from the dish, then decorate all over with the whipped cream and arrange a ring of glacé cherries with nuts and grated chocolate in the centre. Serve chilled. Serves 8 to 12.

'A Proud Mother'

Pineapple Dessert

A party gateau incorporating crushed pineapple with sponge cakes and cream.

1 tablespoon gelatine	**2 eggs, separated**
16 fl.oz milk	**1 tin crushed pineapple, drained**
2 oz sugar	**10 fl.oz whipped cream**

Packet of boudoir biscuits

DECORATION

6 pineapple rings   6 glacé cherries

First, soften the gelatine in 4 fl.oz of the cold milk. Scald the rest of the milk in a pan, remove from the heat, add the gelatine milk and stir until dissolved. Beat the sugar and egg yolks together in a bowl, stir in a little of the hot milk and then return this mixture to the milk in the pan. Cook, stirring, over a very low heat for about 5 minutes and then set aside the custard to cool. When the custard begins to set, add the crushed pineapple and fold in 7 fl.oz of the whipped cream and the stiffly beaten egg whites. Lightly butter a rectangular dish approx. 6 x 10 inches and 2 inches deep and line the bottom with boudoir biscuits. Pour over half the pineapple mixture. Arrange another layer of biscuits and finish with the rest of the mixture. Refrigerate overnight. Next day, turn out the gateau on to a serving dish and decorate with the remaining cream, the pineapple rings and glacé cherries. Serves 6.

Apple Meringue

An orange flavoured apple base with a meringue topping.

1 lb Bramley apples, peeled, cored and sliced
Sugar to taste   Zest of 1 orange   2 eggs, separated
4 oz caster sugar

Set oven to 300° F or Mark 2. Butter a deep pie dish. Rinse the apple segments in cold water and put into a pan with sufficient sugar to taste. Stew gently, stirring occasionally, until reduced to a pulp. Allow to cool and then stir in the orange zest and the two egg yolks and put into the dish. To make the meringue, whisk the egg whites stiffly, add half the caster sugar and whisk again until the mixture holds its peaks. Finally, fold in the remaining caster sugar. Spread the meringue over the apple mixture and bake for about 1 hour until browned on top. Serve cold with whipped cream. Serves 4.

METRIC CONVERSIONS

The weights, measures and oven temperatures used in the preceding recipes can be easily converted to their metric equivalents. The conversions listed below are only approximate, having been rounded up or down as may be appropriate.

Weights

Avoirdupois	Metric
1 oz.	just under 30 grams
4 oz. (¼ lb.)	app. 115 grams
8 oz. (½ lb.)	app. 230 grams
1 lb.	454 grams

Liquid Measures

Imperial	Metric
1 tablespoon (liquid only)	20 millilitres
1 fl. oz.	app. 30 millilitres
1 gill (¼ pt.)	app. 145 millilitres
½ pt.	app. 285 millilitres
1 pt.	app. 570 millilitres
1 qt.	app. 1.140 litres

Oven Temperatures

	°Fahrenheit	Gas Mark	°Celsius
Slow	300	2	150
	325	3	170
Moderate	350	4	180
	375	5	190
	400	6	200
Hot	425	7	220
	450	8	230
	475	9	240

Flour as specified in these recipes refers to plain flour unless otherwise described.